Walk with Me

Robyn Forbes

BookLeaf
Publishing

Presentation by *BookLeaf Publishing*

Web: www.bookleafpub.com

E-mail: info@bookleafpub.com

ISBN: 9789395890274

First edition 2022

DEDICATION

For my BabyBug, you deserve the world - I love you to the moon and back. I have been beyond blessed being your mother, you are the greatest gift God could have given me.

ACKNOWLEDGEMENT

This book wouldn't have happened if it weren't for my friend Justine; who pushed me to try and listened as I wracked my brain and panicked every second of the way. Very few knew what I was doing; but, she held my hand (through messenger) on the entire journey.

The journey I am on is filled with people who deserve so much more than a thank you.

My parents were the safe haven to run to - they dropped everything to come get me when I finally admitted the worst was happening. Helped me with anything and everything, from babysitting to food and everything in between.

Tierayn, who literally held my hand, hugged me and supported me through leaving, going to the police, fighting in court and then testifying.

Aunt Edna & Uncle Gordie, who spent countless hours helping watch my daughter when I had to work or just being ears to listen as I waded through everything.

Uncle Steven, who came running with Dad to pick me up and be an extra source of strength when I had very little left.

Clarissa, one of the best friends a girl could find; moving home brought us into each other's life - God certainly had an interesting plan for that. We're just two single moms who do life together. I don't know how I would do some of the things I do without you; thanks for reminding me that I am beautiful and it's ok to take a minute for myself.

G, my friend, I am sorry that you know all too well what my journey is like. Thank you for all your help as I spammed your phone asking for re-reads and edits!

Erica, who spent hours going through the edits with me and cheering me on straight through to the deadline.

I'm grateful every day for everyone in my life, there is no way I could list each and every person who has helped and supported me. I thank God every day that He put you on my path. Without Him, I would absolutely not have found healing and peace.

PREFACE

The journey this book takes was long and hard. It is by no means over; however, God, and a lot of people, walked it with me. I hope they know how important they are. This is not a walk with sunshine and roses, there is a deep well of darkness it trudges through. I hope all that read it can feel the emotions expressed in every line. As Annie sang “the sun will come out tomorrow”, some days that's the only thing to cling to - that tomorrow is a better day; God willing.

Frame a Narrative

Every life has a start,
there is always an end.
The narrative is in between;
it's the meat on the bone,
the truth to be shared.

My narrative twists,
it turns. It began in love;
then rooted in heartbreak,
tears, manipulation of my brain,
and of what I once thought was love.

My narrative speaks of betrayal,
the breaking of my spirit,
and the shattering of my heart
At the hand of a man I loved.
A man who swore to love me.

My narrative speaks of another betrayal.
It speaks of who I called friend,
rewriting the narrative, creating fictional circumstances,
attempting to defend and excuse my abusers' actions.
It speaks of their attempts to discourage me, to overshadow my narrative.

My narrative speaks of rebuilding,
lack of faith in humanity.
It speaks of the challenge facing the world,
and taking step after step,
on the slow walk from victim to survivor.

Life is framing the narrative.
Telling my truth when I struggled to breathe;
overcoming the pain and trauma.
Framing the narrative is necessary,
Sharing the truth lived and born through perseverance,
and a deep faith.

My narrative has now twisted again;
Still rocky, sometimes painful, still ever true.
It still screams with the trauma, heartbreak and pain;
It also shines brightly with love, deep and strong faith.

Filling the space between the start and end;
that's where you find the truth, that's where you find life.

All I wanted

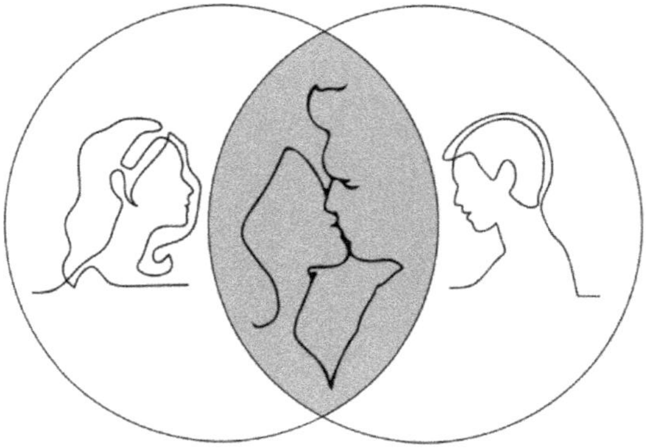

It was like freefalling,
air rushed from my lungs,
colours were bright and beautiful.

It was like dancing,
upbeat and happy,
constant motion.

It was like a cup of tea,
calm and warm,
beautiful comfort.

It was like ice cream,
delicious and sweet,
something I wanted more of.

Loving you was all I wanted.

When the people are gone

When people are around, you would say
Gosh, you are so beautiful! I love you so much!
But, when the people are gone, you quietly say
I want you to be healthy, maybe you should lose
weight.

When people are around, you would say
You're doing so well with your new trainer
Beautiful, why don't I make supper.
But, when the people are gone, you quietly say
Eating off-plan won't hurt for a day!

When people are around, you would say
Don't forget how beautiful you are!
But, when the people are gone, you quietly say

Baby, I want you around for a long time, why don't you lose some weight?

When people are around, you would say
You got rid of your trainer? Why? You were doing so well.
But, when the people are gone, you angrily say
Babe, we can't afford the trainer - even with you working 2 jobs and me 1.

When people are around, you would say
Babe, you are so beautiful!
But, when the people are gone, you quietly say
I want you to be around for a long time; maybe you should lose some weight.

When people are around, you would say
It's amazing how great you balance your jobs and being a wife and mother.
But, when the people are gone, you angrily say
What do you mean you are tired? You're just a mom and you only work 2 jobs.

When people are around, you would say
You should go back to Girl Guides; you love it so much!
But, when the people are gone, you angrily say
Why aren't you doing more at home? Something is going to have to go.

When people are around, you would say
You're such a good mom to our daughter!
But, when the people are gone, you quietly say
You don't spend enough time with your
daughter.

When people are around, you would say
Don't forget how beautiful you are!
But, when the people are gone, you quietly say
Baby, I want you around for a long time, why
don't you lose some weight?

He didn't

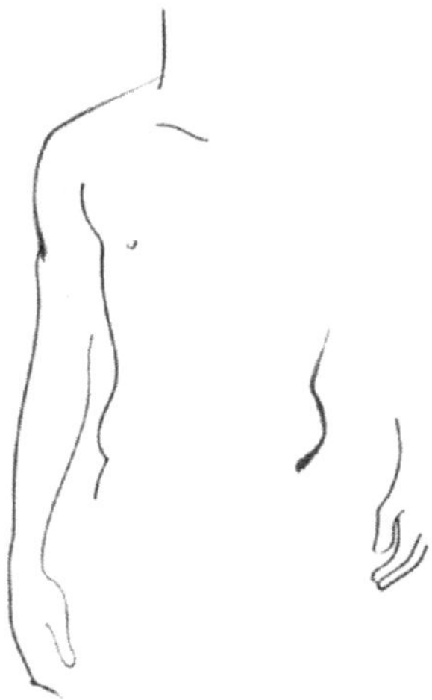

Washing the dishes,
my back to the kitchen.
He pins me to the sink,
he gropes me,
I beg him to stop.
He didn't.

Reading bedtime stories,
our daughter, right there next to me.
His hand snakes into my bra,
I bat his hands,
plead with him to stop!
He didn't.

Reading my book;
he keeps nuzzling my chest,
hands creeping below my waist.
Asking him to stop,
he didn’t.

He pulls at my clothes,
grabs my butt,
ignores my space,
pleading with him to stop.
He didn’t.

Exhausted,
asleep earlier than normal.
Woken up to him above me.
Pleading for him to stop,
He didn’t.

View from the stand

Hard wood, covered in fake leather,
plexiglass and a microphone;
keeping me surrounded
and broadcasting my shame and humiliation.

Sitting there, trying not to fidget,
looking anywhere but at him.
Waiting for the questions,
trying to keep breathing.

The prosecutor, she lays the scene;
she tells the backstory,
asks me to tell all the lurid details.
Breaking down every single second,
describing each movement, each word;
verbalizing the worst moments I've ever had

The defense, they go on the attack.
Breaking down every word, each sentence;

Rehashing and rephrasing everything,
Trying to trip me up, trying to make me lie.

Why did you go to the police?
Is it possible that he didn't understand you didn't
want him to touch you?
But, why did you go to the police?
You say you loved him - why go to the police?
Are you sure he knew you wanted him to stop?

Hard wood, covered in fake leather;
plexiglass and a microphone,
Keeping me surrounded,
and broadcasting my survivor story.

Once upon a time

Once upon a time, you were my friend;
you had my back and I had yours.
Once upon a time, I had faith in you;
you seemed a great person to be around.

Once upon a time, you introduced me to him;
unknown to me, helping set the tone of my
marriage.
Once upon a time I helped raise your child;
I love him, still, as though I birthed him.

Once upon a time you helped break me;
You defended him, raised him up.
Once upon a time, you tried to say you helped
me;
you told everyone you were in my corner

Once upon a time, I loved you like a sister,
until I saw the truth.

Once upon a time, I saw you were a boogie man,
You haunted my nightmares.

Once upon a time, I saw my world topple;
Fell further under as your betrayal shook me.
Once upon a time, I thought maybe I was wrong;
You broke that hope.

Once upon a time, I believed in fairy tales.

Remember it all

I can still remember the butterflies in my
stomach,
the heat from my green tea with raspberry,
the softness of the leather chair I sat in.

I can still remember the joy,
the sheer excitement I felt,
that you returned my interest.

I still remember that first look,
the tightness of my chest,
as I tried to breathe, meeting you the first time.

I can still feel our first kiss,
the surprise I felt at how quickly I fell;

I can still see that look on your face,
when I told you that I loved you for the first time.

I can still see, hear, feel it all.
That's why it's so hard,
knowing that you would ruin that all.

It makes it so confusing,
all that history mixing with the present.
The joy, laughter and love,
mingling with the toxic sadness and
immeasurable pain.

I can still remember it all;
most times now,
I wish I could forget.

Still mine

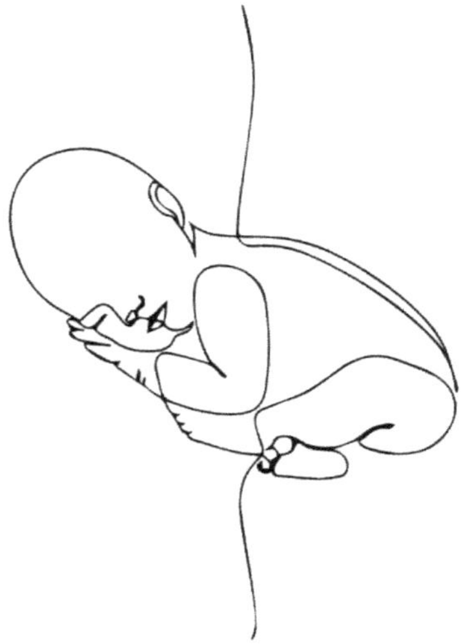

I wasn't there when you drew your first breath,
but I was, when your sister drew hers.
Her first breath, stole mine away;
the look on your face when you first saw her,
stole it again.

I didn't birth you, I didn't see your first steps;
hear your first words or first laugh.
Those that I have witnessed and felt,
those precious sounds - echo in my heart.

I didn't want to go away from you,
I didn't want to hurt you.
I have no legal claim to you,
I have no rights to you.

However, you are still mine - through the core.
In my heart and in my soul.
You are still mine.

You likely won't speak to me again,
Know I love you - even if you don't want it.
Know I'm here, if you ever need me.
I didn't leave you - I left him.
You are still mine.

Every day, every second,
You are still mine - even if you never
acknowledge me.

They all ask

Why, they all ask, didn't you leave?
Because maybe it's my own fault.

Why, they all ask, did you stay?
Because maybe it's all in my head.

Why, they all ask, didn't you ask for help?
Because then, it's real.

Why, they all ask, did you let him do that to
you?
Because, at first I didn't see. Then, I was scared.

Why, they all ask, would you take it?
Because it became normal, it was my life.

Why, they all ask, don’t you move on?
Because, my marriage was traumatic.

Why, they all ask, don’t you just get over it?
Because, abuse changed my brain. I'm relearning life.

Why, they all ask.

Prison Door

There's a social acceptance,
a cultural norm,
perpetuating the cycle;
creating more victims.

We pretend it's ok,
don't talk about reality.
Let everyone think marriage,
removes consent.

Marriage is not permission,
it is not ownership;
yet, we treat it that way;
"They're married!" is the defence.

We don’t talk about the abuse,
the intentional ignorance of choice;
let’s just pretend,
that spouses can’t say no.

Marriage is a vow,
to support, love, care, encourage.
It's not blanket consent,
it's not a pass to abuse.

Looking back,
that social acceptance,
the cultural norm,
was my prison door.

Steps

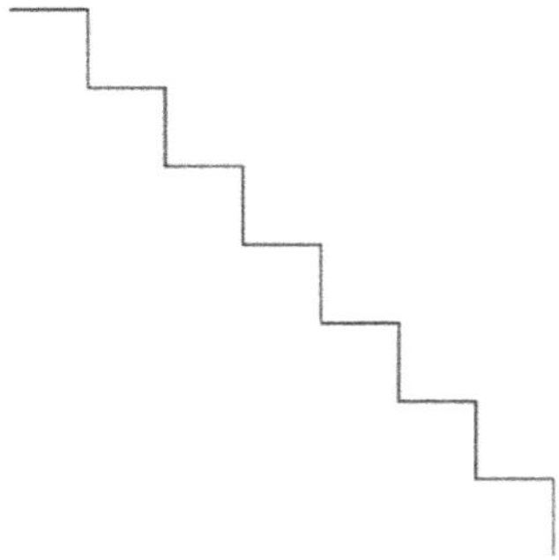

1:
Admit it happened
Go to the police,
Give a statement,
Get somewhere safe.

2:
Get a lawyer,
Explain the custody concerns,
File applications,
File amendments

3:
Family Court
Have the judge say "why did you leave?"

"He's not proven guilty"
"Leaving hurt your daughter, you should have stayed"

4:
Court Prep
Review the statement,
Prosecutor offers to cancel the case,
Understand the odds are not to the victim.

5:
Testify
Sit on the stand,
Tell the truth
Face the defence, as they shred your reputations

6:
Wait for the court date,
Wait for the decision,
Wait for the sentencing.

7:
Appeal date set,
Countdown the days,
Fully recount the trial,
Wait for a decision

8:
Keep moving,
Keep stressing,
Keep waiting
Appeal Dismissed.

Lost

Have you ever lost yourself,
so deep into the darkness,
that you couldn't find yourself?
You couldn’t decide the little things,
which toothpaste,
which shampoo?

Have you ever lost yourself,
so far behind,
that you didn’t know what you liked?
You couldn’t choose the meal,
the colour,
the book?

Have you ever lost yourself,
so deep in the sadness,
you can’t find joy?
You couldn’t find the laughter,
the smiles,
the humour?

Have you ever lost yourself?

Second to Second

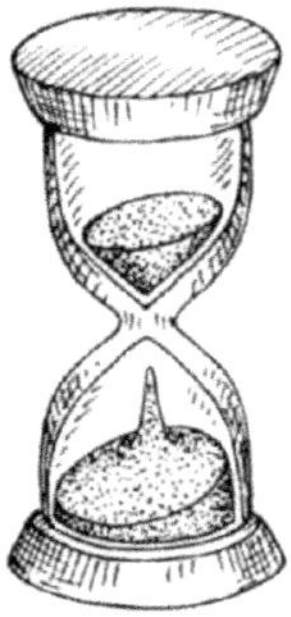

One second I'm fine,
the world is good.
Flowers grow, the clouds are sparse
and there's hope for tomorrow

One second I'm fearful
the world is scary.
Flowers will die, the sun burns
and there's too much unknown for tomorrow.

One second I'm apathetic
the world is ok.
Flowers are there, it will rain or it will shine,
and tomorrow is still tomorrow.

One second I'm great,
the world is beautiful.

Flowers bloom, the sun shines
and tomorrow looks fantastic.

Second to second,
day to day,
emotions change the view.
Life is all ebb and flow.

Unspoken prayer

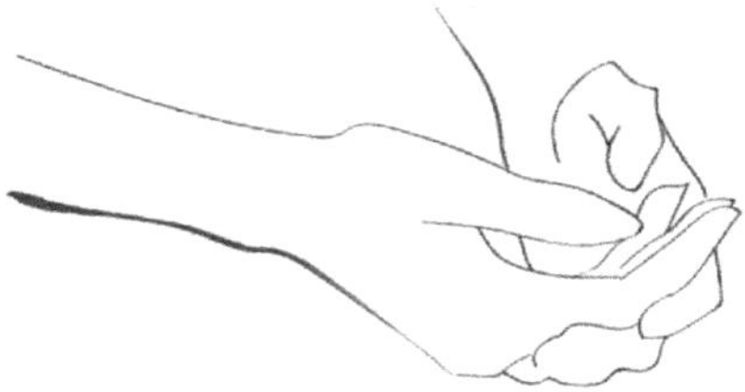

I'm all apart,
Broken pieces scattered around.
Shattered soul shards,
Littering the floor.

Do you know the challenge,
The dark holes and scary places?
Do you know I'm not whole,
I'm chaos on a spin?

Utterly in awe,
shaken to the core;
as God sent you in my direction,
He answered an unspoken prayer.

You swept in,
Changed the tone,
Made me remember myself
And told me I am enough.

You reminded me of the small bits;
the lost and tired parts of me,
that I let go of when I shattered.

Walk away

Before you tell me what to think...
take a breath,
a deep breath;
then walk away.

Before you tell me what to feel...
Breathe deeply in your nose,
out your mouth
then, walk away.

Before you tell me what to do...
take a minute of self-reflection,
ask yourself do I want your input?
Then, walk away

My thoughts, heart and actions
they come from me and where I've walked.
They are authentic, gritty and raw.

Before you try to tell me,
walk away.

Made Stronger

When ceramic shatters, a tapestry tears,
a coffee mug cracks and a mirror breaks,
that's not the end of its story.

Someone can take all those shattered,
broken pieces
and make new beautiful art.

One simply has to look around them,
the beautiful patchwork quilts and tiled tables;
made from the scraps and broken pieces of the
world.

Though you broke me,
shattered pieces of me and tore parts of me to
shreds,
I was put back together, remade, and repurposed.

Made stronger
and more beautiful
than ever.

If & When

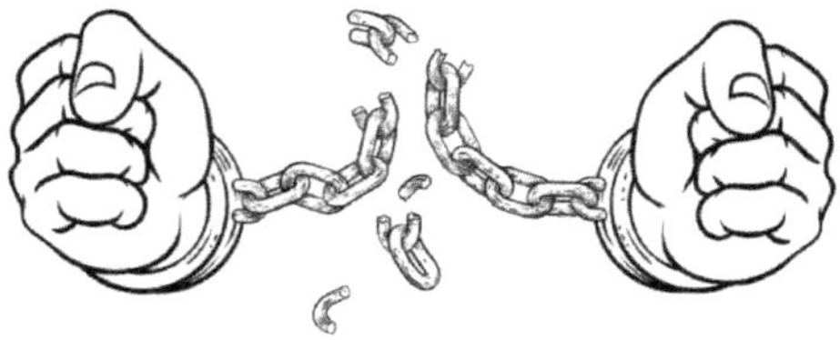

If I leave,
she will suffer.
She will be stuck between us,
separated continually and forced to lose out.

If I leave,
I could lose her.
I could lose my career,
and lose my meagre savings.

If I leave,
people may not believe me.
The courts could say I was wrong,
The world could shun me.

When I left,
She did suffer.
But I was there,
I held her and soothed her.

When I left,
I lost my job,
I had to use my savings.
But we were safe,
I can rebuild.

When I left,
Some believed, some didn't.
Criminal court believed me,
Family court waffled.

When I left,
the fears of "if I leave",
came to fruition.

When I left,
I started over.
She thrived, she continues to thrive.
Because I left.

Rebuild

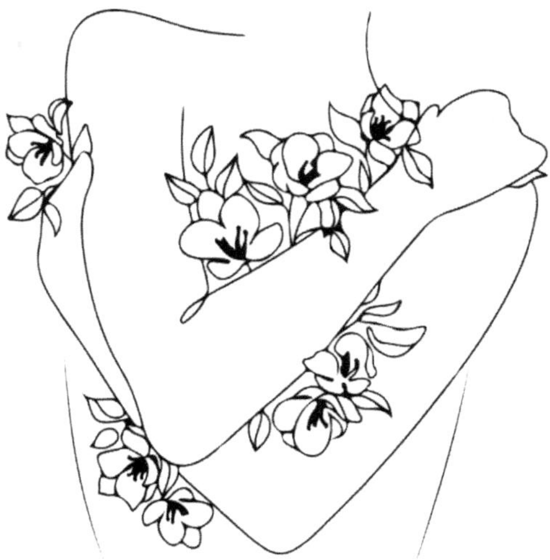

Building a house,
It takes time,
There are always delays.

Losing a house,
That can take seconds,
A blink of an eye.

Rebuilding a life,
That takes strength, patience,
Great amounts of faith.

A foundation can be shaken,
It can be cracked,
But it can be strengthened.

Every shake my life took,
Every crack that appeared,
Was filled and strengthened with faith

The rebuild took time,
Tears, pain and time.
The results,
Are beyond beautiful.

If you're reading this

If you're reading this,
and it all sounds too familiar;
I'm sorry you relate,
but remember,
you're not alone.

If you're reading this,
and it sounds like your life,
I'm sorry you relate.
when you are ready, ask for help.
it's OK if it takes you time.

If you're reading this
and it sounds like your past;

I’m sorry you relate,
but I’m glad you’re out.
I pray you're healing.

If you’re reading this,
and you can’t relate,
I’m so grateful.
I pray you can never relate.

A letter to him

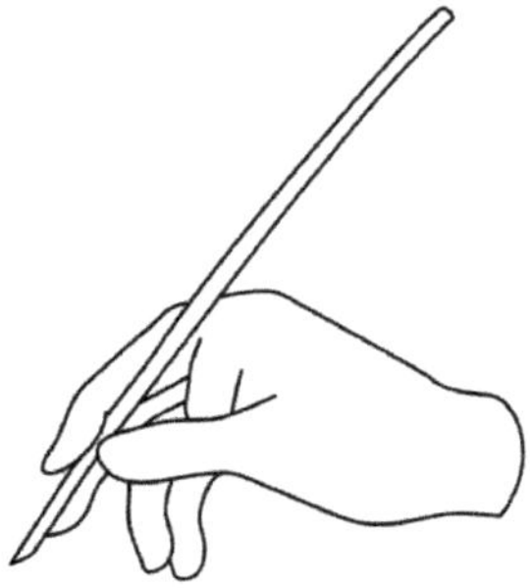

If you ever read this,
know that this book,
isn’t about you.

If you ever read this,
know that you broke me,
but not irreparably.

If you ever read,
know that I didn't need you,
I'm better off.

If you’re reading this,
know that I overcame you,
I am undefeated.

www.ingramcontent.com/pod-product-compliance
Lightning Source LLC
Chambersburg PA
CBHW051741130826
49812CB00033B/956
9789395890274